The Critter Saver Handbook

MW01518571

Saving Species Today,
because tomorrow is too late!

Enjoy your day and the world around you!™

By C S Wurzberger, the Critter Saver

Want to use this Critter Saver Handbook curriculum in your school, home schooling group, summer camp, daycare center, library, church, girl & boy scouts, 4-h group, campground, zoo, aquarium, wildlife conservation center, or other?

Contact us at Office@AwesomeAnimalAcademy.org for bulk order quantities and discounts.

ISBN: 9798877985865

Awesome Animal Academy
C S Wurzberger, the Critter Saver
P. O. Box 343
Marlboro, VT 05344

AwesomeAnimals.org

AwesomeAnimalAcademy.org

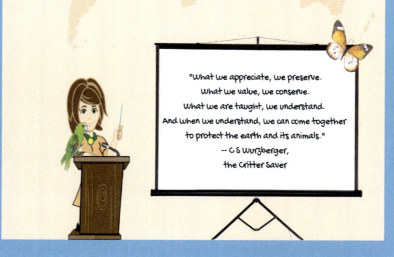

"What we appreciate, we preserve.
What we value, we conserve.
What we are taught, we understand.
And when we understand, we can come together
to protect the earth and its animals."
-- C S Wurzberger,
the Critter Saver

This Handbook is dedicated to
the Dodo Bird.
May you inspire the next generation
of young people to launch and lead their
own Critter Saver Project™ so no more
animals go extinct!

Dear Critter Saver Champion,

Welcome to the wild world of saving species!

I'm C S Wurzberger, but my friends call me CS the Critter Saver. I specialize in helping people like you launch conservation projects around the world.

First, I'd like to share a story with you that profoundly set the course for my life and why I've written this fun-filled Field Guide series for you.

It all started when I was 10 years old!

I was asked to select an animal and write a paper for my English class. As I was flipping through the pages and pictures of a book, I came across the Dodo bird, a funny looking creature that caught my attention.

As I read on, I discovered that the Dodo bird went extinct in 1681 because of over-hunting and the introduction of animals that preyed on its young.

Boy, was I an upset little girl! I thought, 'This bird could have been saved if people had cared a little more.'

I remember coming home from school to tell my parents about the tragic news, yet they didn't seem to understand why I was so upset. I stomped my feet and shouted, "But we need to care. This bird will never be seen on the Earth again!"

It was hard for me to understand why no one in my life seemed to care about my love for animals. I was a quiet, shy little girl and I didn't have the confidence and courage to speak up.

Well, now I do!

I spend my time passionately speaking up for animals and mentoring young people like you who want to make a difference in our world!

I don't want to see any more animals going extinct!

Most importantly, I'm here to help you gain the confidence, courage, and resources you need to speak up and protect the animals you love!

C S, the Critter Saver

NOTE to Parents & Educators:

Something amazing happens to young people in the presence of animals.

They feel calmer, more curious, and more joyful. Plus, animals support a young person's emotional health by giving unconditional love, comfort, security, and teaches them about compassion, empathy, and responsibility.

But simply being around animals is not enough. It is important for them to also care for the animals in a way that will have a real impact and protect them.

Help them engage in species-saving projects and become a Critter Saver Champion™.

TABLE OF CONTENTS

GET READY TO JOIN OTHER ANIMAL-LOVERS FROM

around the globe who are leading projects that are:

- Saving bees by planting pollinator gardens,
- Eliminating the use of plastic bags to help save sea turtles,
- Avoiding foods that contain palm oil in order to help save orangutans,
- And so much more!

►►► WITH MY BACKGROUND AS A CONSERVATION LEADERSHIP COACH...

educator, and podcaster, I'm here to help mission-driven animal-lovers like you lead and launch your own Critter Saver Project™.

Anything you're passionate about can be turned into a project that shares your concerns — and brings your ideas and solutions to the world!

It is important to save species today, because tomorrow is too late!

►►► LET'S BEGIN WITH THE ANIMAL YOU WANT TO PROTECT!

It's easy! This interactive Handbook will walk you through each step and give you a fun, detailed direction to follow.

So, let's get started!

INTRODUCTION

Enjoy your step-by-step path to
protecting the animals you love!

Connect

Care

Champion

HOW TO USE THIS HANDBOOK

Welcome to the "Critter Saver Handbook"!

Here is your chance to help protect the animals you love while also growing your leadership skills, building confidence, and expanding your entrepreneurial thinking.

This guide is designed to help you, your family, friends, and classmates connect with, care for, and champion the animals you love and the ones you have yet to meet.

It's easy! This interactive, project-based handbook will guide you through each step and give you fun, detailed directions to launch your own Critter Saver Project™ and join the Critter Saver Champions™!

So, get ready to jumpstart your journey into wildlife conservation and join other animal lovers from around the globe who are leading projects that are:
- Saving Monarchs by planting milkweed gardens,
- Eliminating the use of plastic bags to help save sea turtles,
- And so much more!

Have fun saving bees to butterflies, wildlife to sea life, and exotic to endangered!

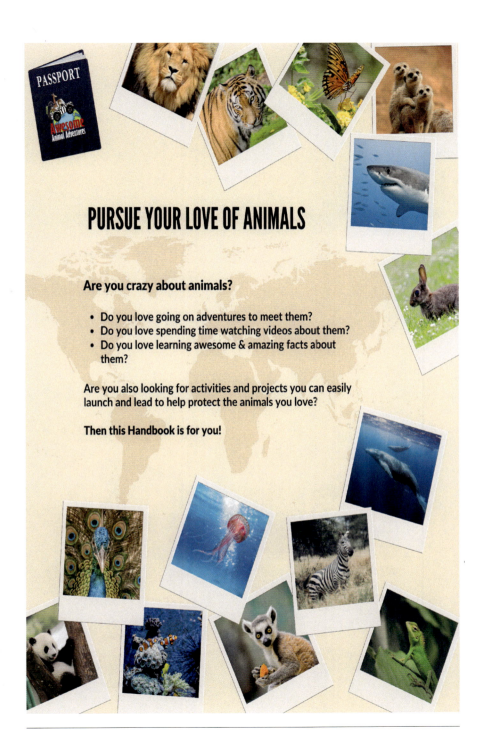

PURSUE YOUR LOVE OF ANIMALS

Are you crazy about animals?

- Do you love going on adventures to meet them?
- Do you love spending time watching videos about them?
- Do you love learning awesome & amazing facts about them?

Are you also looking for activities and projects you can easily launch and lead to help protect the animals you love?

Then this Handbook is for you!

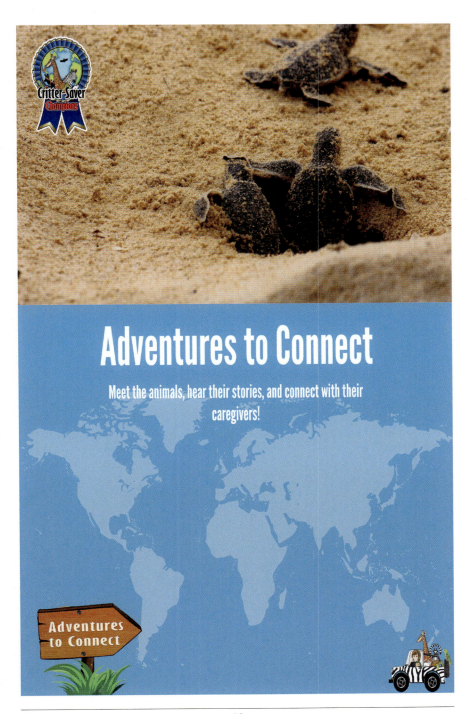

Adventures to Connect

Meet the animals, hear their stories, and connect with their caregivers!

STEP 1: PICK AN ANIMAL TO PROTECT

Here is your chance to dive into the world of Awesome Animals.

In this Step you'll:

- 1-1 Choose your animal
- 1-2 Draw a picture of your animal
- 1-3 Explore where they live in the wild
- 1-4 Explore where they live in captivity
- 1-5 Look up some wild, wonderful, and wacky facts
- 1-6 Write a tale about your critter's day
- Summary – Action Steps
- Things I learned in this section
- Notes

PICK AN ANIMAL TO PROTECT

Choose your animal

There are many animals that need your help!

GROUP 1:
Some are wild animals who are being harmed by too much pollution, habitat loss, or poaching, others are farm animals who are suffering from overcrowding on factory-style farms.

GROUP 2:
There are also Heritage Breeds of livestock that are going extinct because not enough farmers are raising them.

GROUP 3:
Plus, homeless pets like cats and dogs living on the streets or in local animal shelters.

GROUP 4:
There are even animals in your community that really need your help.

The more you learn about animals and the issues that affect them, the more you can do to help care for them.

Here is your chance to share your concerns and solutions with the world!

Choose an animal and take the first step in sharing your action plan to protect them.

The more you care, the more effective you will be in helping others to care, also.

AwesomeAnimals.org

PICK AN ANIMAL TO PROTECT

Now it's time to pick one animal to focus on for
this Critter Saver Project™.

*Note: You can always come back and create additional projects
for each animal you love.*

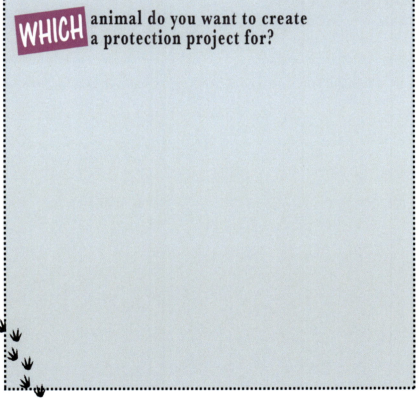

WHICH animal do you want to create
a protection project for?

PICK AN ANIMAL TO PROTECT

Draw a picture of your animal or print one out and glue it here.

Now let's have some fun discovering more about the animal you chose!
Search online or hop down to your local library.

AwesomeAnimals.org

PICK AN ANIMAL TO PROTECT

Explore where they live in the wild

Where do you live in the world?

_____

Where does the animal live in?

_____

Color in where you live and with a different color where the animal lives.

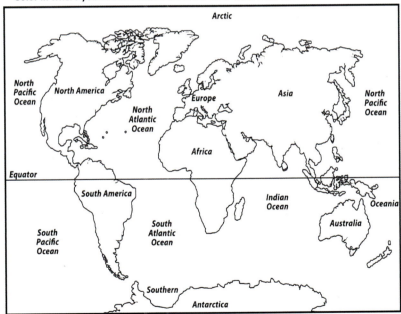

PICK AN ANIMAL TO PROTECT

Explore where they live in the captivity

What zoos, aquariums, wildlife parks, sanctuaries or other places do they live?

_____

_____

_____

SCAN ME

With adult permission you can also search our online zoo directory: VisitAwesomeAnimals.com

PICK AN ANIMAL TO PROTECT

Look up some wild and wacky facts

What Makes Your Critter Extra Special? What are some of their unique traits, sounds they make, or ways they help the ecosystem they live in? Where do they live, what do they eat, what is their family unit, and more.

What does the animal look like? (color, fur, feathers, etc)	How big are they?
How long do they live for?	**What is their lifecycle?**
Describe their family unit? (alone, with family, etc)	
What do they eat? Where do they get their food?	**How do they communicate?**

List more wild and wacky facts

What other wild & wacky facts did you discover?

List your resources:

PICK AN ANIMAL TO PROTECT

Write a tale about your critter's day

Have fun writing a story about the animal you chose. Imagine what their day is like. What do they do, what do they eat, who do they spend time with? Let your imagination go wild!

Summary - Action Steps

STEP 1: Pick An Animal To Protect

Mark off each item on the checklist to ensure you are moving closer to bringing your Critter Saver Project to life:

- ☐ I have chosen an animal I want to protect.

- ☐ I have drawn a picture of the animal I chose.

- ☐ I have explored where they live in the wild.

- ☐ I have explored where they live in the captivity.

- ☐ I have looked up some wild & wacky facts like where it lives, what it eats, and more fun things.

- ☐ I wrote a story about my critter's day

Congratulations! Now you're ready to move on to STEP 2: PLAN how you can help protect your animals.

Things I learned in this section

_____

_____

_____

_____

_____

_____

_____

_____

_____

_____

_____

_____

_____

_____

_____

_____

My Notes

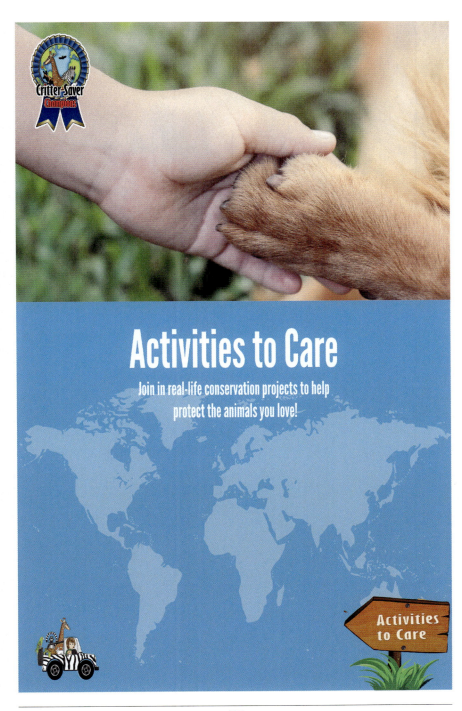

Activities to Care

Join in real-life conservation projects to help
protect the animals you love!

Activities
to Care

STEP 2: PLAN How You Can Help Protect Them

Now that you're done picking an animal you love, it's time to roll up your sleeves and explore how you can help.

In this Step you'll:

- 2-1 Discover how many live in the world
- 2-2 Uncover the issues impacting their lives
- 2-3 Walk in your critter's paws, fins, etc.
- 2-4 Map out your mission to help.
- Summary – Action Steps
- Things I learned in the section
- Notes

PLAN HOW YOU CAN HELP PROTECT THEM

Discover how many live in the world

Is their population growing, staying the same, or falling (going extinct)?

To make your research time easier, here are two organizations that track the population status of species around the world and in the U.S.

(If you live outside of the U.S. simply search for the organization that monitors your country.)

IUCN Red List of Threatened Species™

IUCN Species Survival Commission has been counting the status of species, on a global scale for the past 50 years. Visit their IUCN Red List of Threatened Species™ http://www.iucnredlist.org

U.S. Fish & Wildlife Service

In the United States there is also the U.S. Fish & Wildlife Service. They are the main federal partner responsible for administering the Endangered Species Act (ESA). https://www.fws.gov/endangered/

Research Notes:

What did you discover?

STEP 2-1

PLAN HOW YOU CAN HELP PROTECT THEM

Discover how many live in the world

Is their population growing, staying the same, or falling (going extinct)?

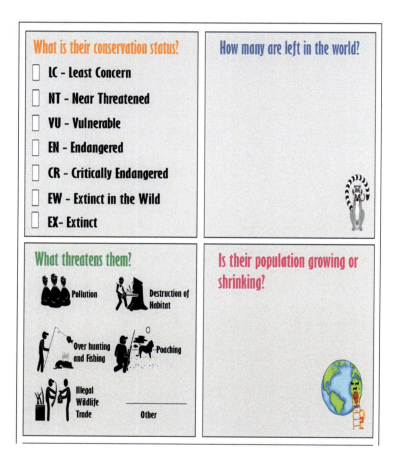

What is their conservation status?

☐ LC – Least Concern

☐ NT – Near Threatened

☐ VU – Vulnerable

☐ EN – Endangered

☐ CR – Critically Endangered

☐ EW – Extinct in the Wild

☐ EX – Extinct

How many are left in the world?

What threatens them?

Pollution

Destruction of Habitat

Over hunting and Fishing

Poaching

Illegal Wildlife Trade

Other

Is their population growing or shrinking?

AwesomeAnimals.org

PLAN HOW YOU CAN HELP PROTECT THEM

Uncover the issues impacting them

Why does this animal need your help? Is it dealing with habitat loss, pollution, poachers, or other things? Check off the ones you think apply:

Identify Issues

- ☐ HABITAT CHANGES
- ☐ OVER HARVESTING
- ☐ CLIMATE CHANGE
- ☐ PESTISICES
- ☐ SPREAD OF DISEASES
- ☐ POLLUTION
- ☐ NON NATIVE SPECIES
- ☐ POACHERS

PLAN HOW YOU CAN HELP PROTECT THEM

Uncover the issues impacting them

What other things are impacting the animals and their lives?

_____

_____

_____

_____

_____

_____

_____

_____

_____

_____

PLAN HOW YOU CAN HELP PROTECT THEM

Habitat Exploration Project: Uncover the Secrets of Animals' Homes and Habitats

Join this exciting journey and become a wildlife detective. Investigate where your animal lives, what makes their homes special, and how you can help protect them.

From dense forests and deep oceans to scorching deserts and freezing polar regions, every habitat is a world of its own, teeming with incredible creatures and fascinating facts. So, grab your explorer's hat, a magnifying glass, and your curiosity, and let's dive into the wild world of animal habitats!

Have fun answering these groups of questions:

1. Investigate where your animal lives
2. Discover what makes their homes special
3. Learn how to help protect them

REFERENCES

Note the websites you used to find your information.

1.

2.

3.

4.

5.

6.

AwesomeAnimals.org

Investigate where your animal lives :

1. What kind of habitat does this animal live in? (Forest, desert, ocean, etc.)

2. Is this habitat specific to a particular region or country?

3. What other animals share this habitat with my chosen animal?

PLAN HOW YOU CAN HELP PROTECT THEM

1 Investigate where your animal lives:

4. How does the weather and climate in this habitat affect the animal?

5. Are there any plants or trees in this habitat that are crucial for the animal's survival?

PLAN HOW YOU CAN HELP PROTECT THEM

 Discover What Makes Their Homes Special:

1. What special skills or traits does this animal need to live in its home?

2. How does the animal find food and shelter in its habitat?

3. Does the animal migrate or hibernate depending on the seasons?

PLAN HOW YOU CAN HELP PROTECT THEM

2 Discover What Makes Their Homes Special:

4. Are there any predators or dangers the animal faces in its habitat?

5. How does the animal interact with other species in its habitat?

AwesomeAnimals.org

PLAN HOW YOU CAN HELP PROTECT THEM

3 Learn How to Help Protect Them:

1. Is the animal's habitat under threat? If so, what are the main threats?

2. Are there any conservation groups working to protect this animal and its habitat?

3. What actions can you take to help protect this animal and its habitat?

PLAN HOW YOU CAN HELP PROTECT THEM

3 Learn How to Help Protect Them:

4. How does protecting this animal's habitat benefit other species and the environment as a whole?

5. Are there any laws or regulations in place to protect this animal and its habitat?

PLAN HOW YOU CAN HELP PROTECT THEM

Walk in your critter's paws, fins, etc.

This is an exercise in empathy. Sometimes we need to walk in someone else's shoes or in this case paws, fins, etc. to see what is happening in their life and how they feel.

What are their day-to-day challenges, survival techniques, environmental threats and more?

Circle how you think they are feeling today

Why do you think they feel this way?

_____

_____

_____

What can you do to help them feel better?

_____

_____

_____

PLAN HOW YOU CAN HELP PROTECT THEM

Map out your mission to help

Have fun brainstorming all the ways you can help the animal you chose. Create a vision board, set goals, and brainstorm action steps.

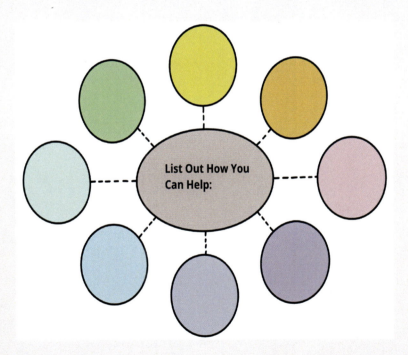

List Out How You Can Help:

PLAN HOW YOU CAN HELP PROTECT THEM

Make a list of all the ways you can help them. Then put a star next to the activity you would like to create your Critter Saver Project™ around:

NOTE: You can always come back and create another project.

- ☐ _____
- ☐ _____
- ☐ _____
- ☐ _____
- ☐ _____
- ☐ _____
- ☐ _____
- ☐ _____
- ☐ _____
- ☐ _____
- ☐ _____
- ☐ _____
- ☐ _____
- ☐ _____

AwesomeAnimals.org

Summary - Action Steps

Plan How You Can Help Protect Them

Mark off each item on the checklist to ensure you are moving closer to bringing your Critter Saver Project™ to life:

☐ I have discovered how many live in the world.

☐ I have uncovered the issues that are impacting them.

☐ I have walked in my critters paws, fins, etc.

☐ I have mapped out my mission to help them.

☐ I have selected my activity to build my Critter Saver Project™ around.

Congratulations! Now you're ready to prepare your Critter Saver Project™.

Things I learned in this section

_____

_____

_____

_____

_____

_____

_____

_____

_____

_____

_____

_____

_____

_____

_____

_____

AwesomeAnimals.org

My Notes

Join the Critter Saver Champions™

A Conservation Club where ambitious and enthusiastic young people come together from around the world to save species, help habitats, and grow leadership skills.

CritterSaverChampions.com

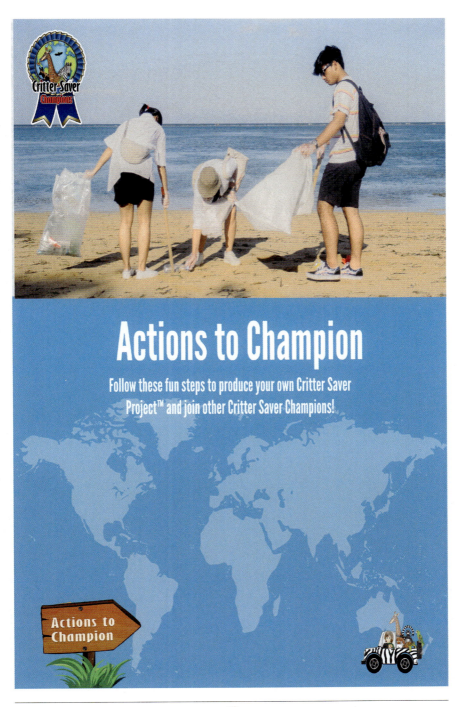

Actions to Champion

Follow these fun steps to produce your own Critter Saver
Project™ and join other Critter Saver Champions!

STEP 3: PRODUCE Your Critter Saver Project™

Now that you're done planning how you can help protect your animal, it's time to create your Critter Saver Project™.

In this Step you'll:

- 3-1 Start your countdown to action
- 3-2 Gather all the details and create your own Critter Saver Project™
- Summary – Action Steps
- Things I learned in the section
- Notes

Start Your Countdown to Action

Narrow down your list of ways to help from the last section and choose one way to focus on right now. (You can always come back to these worksheets and plan additional projects. Maybe you can even enlist your friends and family to join you!)

> **When are you going to kick off your project?**

> **List any notes and needed resources:**

STEP 3-2

PRODUCE YOUR CRITTER SAVER PROJECT™

Gather all the details and create your project

How exciting! This is where you pull all of your work together and create one easy-to-follow Critter Saver Project™ to help protect the animals you love.

Critter Saver Project™

Have fun answering the questions that begin with...
Who - What - Where - When - How

WHAT animal are you helping?

WHAT supplies do you need?

- [ ]
- [ ]
- [ ]
- [ ]

WHEN are you starting your project?

WHAT type of project are you launching?

WHAT is the name of your project?

AwesomeAnimals.org

Critter Saver Project™

Have fun answering the questions that begin with...
Who - What - Where - When - How

WHERE is your project happening?

Example: park, zoo, forest, your house, etc.

WHO are your team members?

- ☐ _____
- ☐ _____
- ☐ _____
- ☐ _____

HOW much funding do you need? (If any?)

Example: Grow a butterfly garden.

EXPENSES:	
Organic Seeds	$10
Garden Soil	$20
Lumber to make raised beds	$55
TOTAL EXPENSES:	**$85**

EXPENSES:	
TOTAL EXPENSES:	

WHEN are you starting your project?

NOTES:

AwesomeAnimals.org

55

Critter Saver Project™

Have fun answering the questions that begin with...
Who - What - Where - When - How

HOW will you get the word out about the animal you are protecting?

SHARE WITH FRIENDS & FAMILY

☐ **POSTER**
☐ **VIDEO**
☐ **PODCAST**
☐ **OTHER**

NOTES:

List people to connect with:

☐
☐
☐
☐
☐
☐
☐
☐

List organizations to connect with:

☐
☐
☐
☐
☐
☐
☐

AwesomeAnimals.org

Additional Project Notes

Summary - Action Steps

Produce Your Critter Saver Project™

Mark off each item on the checklist to ensure you are moving closer to bringing your Critter Saver Project™ to life:

☐ I have started down my countdown to action.

☐ I have gathered all the details for my project.

☐ I have created my Critter Saver Project™.

Congratulations! You have finished your Critter Saver Project™!

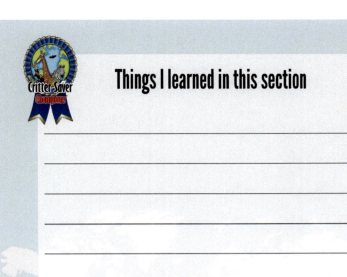

Things I learned in this section

_____

_____

_____

_____

_____

_____

_____

_____

_____

_____

_____

_____

_____

_____

_____

_____

_____

_____

My Notes

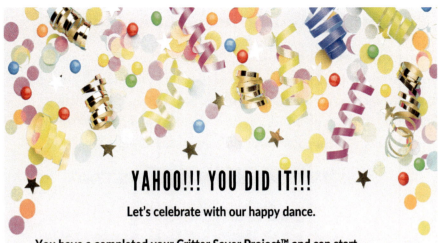

YAHOO!!! YOU DID IT!!!

Let's celebrate with our happy dance.

You have a completed your Critter Saver Project™ and can start protecting the animals you love.

You must be so proud of yourself. I know I sure am proud of you!

Now it's time to PROPEL Your Project Forward and grow your critter superpowers.

Ignite Your Critter Super Powers

Choose from handbooks with a companion video series or live, instructor-led programs (in-person or online) filled with engaging hands-on activities and key lessons in leadership, mastering mindset, confidence building, stewardship, entrepreneurship, podcasting, fundraising, and other awesome topics!

CritterSaverChampions.com

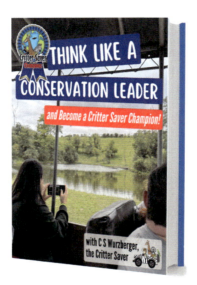

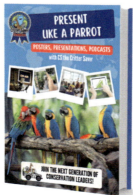

BONUS STEP: PROPEL FORWARD

Ignite your critter super powers and grow confidence, build leadership skills, find fun with fundraising, and more!

Join the Champions!

BONUS STEP: PROPEL Forward

Before you propel forward, take a moment to reflect on your wow moments. learn from your stumbles, and get ready to grow your superpowers.

In this Step you'll:

- 5-1 Cherish your WOW moments
- 5-2 Learn from your stumbles
- 5-3 Explore and choose your next steps
- Summary – Action Steps
- Things I learned in the section
- Notes

Cherish your Wow Moments

Reflect back and record the parts of this project that made you go WOW. For example: a fun fact that caught your attention, etc. Jot them down, draw a picture, or you choose.

What did you enjoy most?	What do you want to do more or?

Show off your Wow Moment!

Learn from your stumbles

Think back. Were there any challenges you faced when working on this Critter Saver Project™? Did you have to do any problem-solving? Jot them down, brainstorm some solutions, and reflect on any lessons you learned.

What challenges did you face?

What solutions did you find?

AwesomeAnimals.org

Explore and choose your next steps

Wow! You've accomplished so much on your journey while building your own Critter Saver Project™. What would you like to learn next?

 I want to learn more about leadership skills.

 I want to learn to present my project with confidence.

 I want to think like a REAL conservation leader.

Be sure to check out all of the Field Guides and Critter Power Programs I've made available for you on my website! AwesomeAnimalAcademy.org

Summary - Action Steps
Propel Forward

Mark off each item on the checklist to ensure you are moving closer to bringing your Critter Saver Project™ to life:

☐ I have cherished my WOW moments.

☐ I have learned from my stumbles.

☐ I am ready to go on to my next steps.

Congratulations! You are a true CRITTER SAVER CHAMPION!

Things I learned in this section

My Notes

Bring a Species Saving Program to Your...

School, homeschooling group, summer camp, library, girl & boy scouts, 4-h group, campground, zoo, aquarium, wildlife conservation center, or any place in the world.

Together, We Can Grow the Next Generation of Conservation Leaders!

CS the Critter Saver travels around the U.S., presenting programs that inspire young people to learn key lessons in leadership, confidence building, stewardship, entrepreneurship, podcasting, and other awesome animal topics!

Let's discuss how the Critter Saver Champions™ curriculum can expand your education programs.

BOOK A CALL TODAY!
AwesomeAnimalAcademy.org

ADDITIONAL RESOURCES

DOUBLE YOUR IMPACT WITH A CONSERVATION COACH

Sign up to work privately with C S the Critter Saver. She is a certified High-Performance Coach ready to tailor each session to your personal goals and aspirations in wildlife conservation. Visit: CStheCritterSaver.com/coaching

VISIT AWESOME ANIMALS (AN ONLINE DIRECTORY)

Here is a fun way to explore Animal-Related Organizations from around the world. Search the most comprehensive online directory of zoos, aquariums, animal sanctuaries, wildlife parks, and conservation organizations available on the Internet. Use the directory for your research projects, homework, vacation planning, job/intern searches, and more!

AwesomeAnimals.org

ABOUT C S Wurzberger, the Critter Saver

> "What we appreciate, we preserve.
> What we value, we conserve.
> What we are taught, we understand.
> And when we understand, we can come
> together to protect the earth and its animals."
> -- C S Wurzberger

CStheCritterSaver.com
AwesomeAnimalAcademy.org

C S Wurzberger, the Critter Saver, is driven by a powerful passion and sense of purpose to help protect our Earth and its animals! She spends her days engaged in, teaching about, and spotlighting species-saving initiatives around the world.

She specializes in working with ambitious and enthusiastic young people who want to launch their own conservation initiatives and socialpreneur projects that protect the animals they animals love while sparking curiosity, building confidence and compassion, growing leadership skills, expanding entrepreneurial thinking, and developing respect and empathy for all!

As a Certified High-Performance Coach, conservation educator, author, podcaster, and presenter with 35+ years of experience, C S offers online and in-person programs at selected youth organizations, summer camps, schools, homeschooling groups, and more.

Plus, in partnership with zoos, aquariums, wildlife conservation centers, farms, and organizations, she provides the curriculum to help expand their conservation programs with Critter Saver *Projects™*.

C S is also the former director of a 150-acre, 300-animal, USDA-licensed petting zoo. There, she created, implemented, and promoted all of their educational programs.

Plus, she experienced the joy of bottle-raising numerous animals such as Walter the Wallaby, Parachute the Field Mouse, Ted the Cheviot Lamb, Andy the Aoudad, and many others critters who touched her heart!

Connect with C S, the Critter Saver by visiting CStheCritterSaver.com & AwesomeAnimalAcademy.org

49360210R00042